Rocked to Sleep Recovery...

the *Pimp-A-Lo* Syndrome
BOOK & WORKBOOK VOL. 2

By: Teena L. Harris

Table of Contents

Rocked to Sleep Recovery
The Pimp-A-Lo Syndrome
Book and Workbook Vol 2

By: Teena L. Harris

Foreword by Bruce George, Co-Founder of Def Poetry Jam

The world we live in is full of people who have been emotionally scorned in their personal, social, and sexual relationships, which makes them become very guarded and untrusting. Going from one bad relationship to another, over a period of time, a person can find themselves playing head games rooted in manipulation for their own selfish gain.

The "Pimp-A-Lo Syndrome" is a cross between a pimp and a gigolo was coined by the author, to describe men who have a pimp mentality with gigolo tendencies. It basically breaks down the interpersonal and social political conditions of people in emotional turmoil. The Pimp-A-Lo Syndrome… the cross between a Pimp and a Gigalo…Volume 1, is a precursor to *Rocked to Sleep Recovery…The Pimp-A-Lo Syndrome Book & Workbook Vol. 2.*

For centuries, philosophers, religious scholars, intellectuals, poets, educators etc… have attempted to gain an understanding on the dynamics of dysfunctional relationships in relation to the conditions that predisposed them. From the Casanova Complex, which is about migratory sexual conquest; to the Cinderella Complex, which describes a woman's fear of independence; to the Peter Pan Syndrome which is about men who are childlike in their relationships, and last but not least the Pimp-A-Lo Syndrome…, which chronicles the Drama Triangle with its Pimp/Gigolo dynamics, they are all attempts at shedding light on how to therapeutically improve and heal the lives of those in interpersonal relationships, that have wounded spirits, which in some cases are rooted in personality disorders.

Rocked to Sleep Recovery…The Pimp-A-Lo Syndrome…Vol 2, delves deeper into the role that women play in the so-called "Pimp-A-Lo Syndrome." In fact the author has also coined the term "Pimp-A-Lette's" to describe how women carry out similar manipulative tactics as men, but from a woman's perspective, to get their needs met. Each syndrome plays on a person's neediness, and breaks down how they manipulate each other for personal gain.

4

What differentiates *Rocked to Sleep...* from other related books about dysfunctional relationships, is the fact that it's less didactic in its approach, as it utilizes a male and female perspective via discussions complete with questions and answers. This makes for an interesting read, as the reader will be able to identify with some if not all of the topics in discussion.

The title *Rocked to Sleep Recovery...*is very relatable in the sense that we can all relate to being rocked to sleep by our primary caretaker albeit a mother, father, grandmother etc... but the author puts a unique spin on the term in terms of a person being rocked into a manipulative situation of circumstance. It's all about using one's assets to control another person. This is not unlike the famed author Robert Greene's book "The Art of Seduction" which is a tool of warfare created by women, to level the playing field with men.

The readers of *Rocked to Sleep Recovery...*will gain a therapeutic perspective on his or her life, as the book breaks down the notion of emotional recovery and relapse. We can all relate to being in dysfunctional relationships, and having to get words of advice from friends or relatives, only to relapse right back into a faulty way of thinking and behaving. This book uses a medical recovery form of intervention, which will give the reader the tools necessary to become more empowered in his/her relationships moving forward.

In *Rocked to Sleep Recovery...*the reader will feel a strong sense of commitment to his/her personal and interpersonal recovery, by utilizing the workbook and inventory guide towards developing a recovery plan. So as you continue reading this book, you will instantaneously feel a strong awareness, of the need for you to change the way you have been operating in your past and current relationships. Enjoy the ride.

Bruce George, Co-Founder of Russell Simmons, Def Poetry Jam on HBO, former Mental Health Clinician.

The Pimp-A-Lo Defined Women Fitting This Role

Chapter 1

Many people were scratching their heads when they saw my first book, **"The Pimp-A-Lo Syndrome; The Cross Between A Pimp & A Gigalo Vol. 1."** Some thought the book was about how to be a pimp or a gigalo. Some were afraid, and some were highly interested to find out about this syndrome, that they had never heard of before, that I coined. However, all of them loved the cover with the sexy red shoes (smiling).

As my book began to circulate, people were completely touched by its contents and many stated that they could most certainly identify with this syndrome, and the dynamics within the book. I discovered that just as many men were interested in the book as women! Please allow me to clarify from the onset: *The Pimp-A-Lo Syndrome* is a unisex issue. While the original definition was outlined in a specific manner in order for me to build a platform, it can apply to either gender. I want to provide my readers with the initial definition, especially those whom may not have read Vol. 1. I would also like to welcome you to get the first volume if you do not have it already.

"A Pimp-A-Lo is a man who has a pimp mentality with gigalo tendencies but is not dedicated to either aspect of the roles. A Pimp-A-Lo is a very confused, insecure man who believes that he will gain his self-worth through utilizing women to fulfill the emotional and spiritual void that he feels. He is an empty person running on "image only." Women are viewed as accomplices and targets to him. A Pimp-A-Lo is a man without a sense of true purpose and he wanders in and out of people's lives (a nomad

of sorts) creating havoc and chaos unbeknownst or knowingly to him" (Harris, 2014). This is just a portion of the main definition of a Pimp-A-Lo from Chapter 4 of my first book. However, I wanted to elaborate more on this definition.

The Pimp-A-Lo could very well be referred to as a *Pimp-A-Lette*. In other words, there are women that have these same behavioral tendencies along with the mentality of using others to feel better about who they are. This syndrome is based on manipulation at the highest level, codependency, and overall emotional abuse of self and others. Some women, just as men do, have deep emotional scars that may have derived from sexual abuse, domestic violence, or family-of-origin messages that set the stage for them to operate in this dysfunctional manner.

I have spoken with hundreds of women that have been sexually abused, still caught-up in the past pain of the severe domestic violence trauma they experienced and they are bitter, making other men pay for their pain. Some of these women were given seriously unhealthy direct messages such as this from their family: ***"You have a money maker between your legs & you better use it!"*** Due to these women being wounded and never truly treating the abuse issues that they have, they use men, or other women to fulfill their needs. They believe that the only thing they have going for themselves is: Great looks, clothing, sex, and a mouthpiece with serious swag. Additionally, if they use this effectively in their own eyes and obtain the score of getting money, or some form of emotional power over a man or a woman they feel superior, but only for a short time frame. Eventually, they too began to decay emotionally, physically and spiritually.

Spiritual Nugget

Let me draw specific attention to the "spirit" that is within a person that operates in this manner. Make no mistake about it this is a spiritual issue just as it is a clinical issue! In the Spirit world manipulation is referred to as "Witchcraft." Since the beginning of time historically, theologically, and physically this type of "spirit" has always existed in human beings. However, it has recently been renamed as, "The Pimp-A- Lo or The Pimp-A-Lette Syndrome." One may want to keep in mind that a person operates out of their "values and morals" which contributes to their standard of living and operating with others. Both men and women have mixed theological beliefs, that may be faulty, and either party can begin to view another living soul, from God, as personal property to be played with or used and ultimately damaged. Thank goodness that God provides healing to those who ask for it and seek it out so that they may heal from the spiritual decay of this syndrome and be set free.

Many of the men that read my first book discussed with me that they experienced women doing these things to them, and it caused them much pain and they had to seek support emotionally and spiritually to heal and get better. Some also reported to me that they were still entrapped with a Pimp-A-Lette. These men said they still had trust issues with women due to their dysfunctional experiences, but they wanted to get past it. There were some men that shared with me that they used to treat women in this unhealthy manner and they were taught this behavior from other men. The men shared that they were even celebrated by other men for using women, and being a player. The women exclaimed pretty much the same thing the men did, and some were currently entangled with a Pimp-A-Lo and they were in tears, but thankful that a healing tool was in place to assist them with beginning to break free and they were glad that someone exposed this syndrome in a honest manner. Then there were women who were just "out-done" and exclaimed, "I will not take myself through any more abuse!" or "I am fine with Jesus alone" or "I am too far in age to tolerate anything from a relationship." However, some that have given up are just wounded, and bitter from the pain left behind from this syndrome. Most people want to be loved, cared for, and treated special no matter what their age. So, the hope is that women and men learn to love and trust again because real love is beautiful.

Ultimately, in order to heal from *The Pimp-A-Lo* or *The Pimp-A-Lette,* one will have to feel, deal, and heal their way through it. I have suggested to many my own experience that may prove to be helpful to them on their respective healing journeys. Locate a clinical therapist and attend all of your sessions, complete any therapeutic assignments given by the therapist, attend support groups, obtain a spiritual guide, change your behavior one action at a time, and lastly detox from the person or persons that you have been doing these behaviors with. Also, if you have a mental health diagnoses please see a medication management provider, and take your medicine as prescribed. ***I totally support mental health treatment.*** As one can see, it really does take "work" to break free. However, the work starts with your willingness.

Now, will you have set-backs & possibly fall off of the bandwagon with your *Pimp-A-Lo* or *Pimp-A-Lette*, or some new similar character? Probably so if you have been deeply engaged in this kind of behavior for a very long time! Yet if you fall off get back on your healing regiment as quickly as possible. We will further discuss relapse, and your recovery plan in chapter 4.

So, to the world, The Pimp-A-Lo Syndrome knows no gender!

The Pimp-A-Lo Syndrome Discussions From Vol. 1

Chapter 2

It was important to me to have active discussions with those who read my book. So, I created a book discussion board for my readers. I wanted to know their thoughts and feelings, and also provide an atmosphere for the mature and serious to talk about real-life relationship issues and healing from brokenness. I informed all of my readers in this book club that I was developing a workbook and their feedback would assist. Let me just say, that some of these discussion questions "blew my wig back" and made me laugh. I also became emotional, and it was healing to me and many others per their own reports in the book group.

In this chapter, we are going to review five of the discussion questions that were **"Sizzling Topics"** in this closed group. In an effort to protect the identity of those in the group, names will not be used. The only name that will be used is mine as the author and facilitator. The other parties will be referred to as "female responder" or "male responder." However, I want you to be assured that these were real discussions, and only small grammatical changes were made for syntax purposes, as some were writing like we talk, which is fine, but it does not go over well in print for a book *(smiles)*.

Discussion Question: Matters of the heart can be very fragile and complicated. These days they nearly have a pill for everything, but they do not have a pill for a broken-heart! That said if your heart has ever "truly" been broken how did you recover from it? What "internal" and "action" steps did you take that assisted you with "pulling through?" Responses to this question may assist someone who is still suffering from a relationship break-up, even if they are no longer physically with the person anymore.

Female Responder: This is an excellent topic. Girl, don't get me started LOL! I had to get with God for real, for real and by getting with God, I got with myself. Deep within myself and started doing me for the first time in my life! I concentrated on accomplishing and completing some positive goals for my LIFE and did! It took my focus off of being broken and hurt. When I started to do positive, estimable things for myself it kept me busy, lifted my spirits, and my self- esteem rose! My sense of self value increased. When I started doing me...it was like...later for feeling bad...I started being real good to myself. When I put the focus on myself and God my life turned around, and I found out life is too short to be anything but happy and that life is good. I became a better person. Nobody has time for that sulking feeling bad stuff and staying stuck in toxic relationships. I started being around positive people who were doing productive things in life. I started aiming at some higher goals and reaching them. I've been writing my own book for ten years ((yeah)) taking my time. I've been stopping here and there over the years and going back in....watch out world, it's coming! I had to pour life back into my spirit, mentally, emotionally and spiritually by incorporating spiritual principles. Like I said, I'd rather feel up then down over the years you learn. I could go on and on...

Male Responder: I think for me and my experience with the broken heart, I had to first understand it wasn't about me. Acceptance of this fact is actually much harder than it seems. The growth from this acceptance is beyond mere mental strength. The growth in the area of acceptance is spiritual. It took some real effort in the area of self awareness. Mostly taking a hard look at how I see myself from the inside. When I got honest and started the process of self acceptance on a deeper level, then and only then was I able to move forward. When I don't see me in a positive light, I will struggle spiritually and emotionally. That took me to the "They decided to move forward and they didn't include me in their plans." Most times, we are quick to start blaming ourselves for the decision of another person. Yeah it hurt, but at least I knew it wasn't about me. There isn't anything wrong with me.

The common thread with the female and male responder to this question was self-realization, spiritual enhancement, and learning how to move forward in life by focusing on achieving other tasks and it assisted them with working through the pain of a broken heart, so that healing could take place. Make no mistake about it, if your heart has truly been broken, or you are deeply disappointed it will take time and active emotional, behavioral, and spiritual work. The answer is most certainly not to get into a romantic relationship with a new person taking your wounded broken heart to them. It is not fair to you, or the new person. So, if your heart is broken pray and get a "recovery plan" to mend your broken heart. Years ago Al Green made a song titled, "How can you mend a broken heart." I loved that song and I still do. The answer to the song is listed above.

Discussion Question: After a period of serious "time" (not 1 week real time) of no interaction at all is it reasonable to be cordial with your ex, or even friends? Cordial doesn't mean sexual, just plain cordial...

Female Responder: I'm friends and or cordial with all my ex's. For some of them it took time, but for most it's a mutual agreement to part and there was a friendship element that we shared, so we normally resume the same behavior minus flirting and expectations. It takes more time for some but adults should be amicable at least.

Male Responder: Yes. I'm friends with all my ex's with the exception of my ex-wife. I have to communicate with her because of the kids. All the others are real cool relationships. As a matter of fact, my ex was the editor of my book.

Female Responder: Tricky question! It depends if you were true friends from the start. It also depends on the nature of the break up! Some break ups you can no longer have any type of dealings. It's best to leave the past in the past. It's a reason why you aren't together.

This discussion question was interesting to say the least. Many said yes, but a few said no. At the end of the day, one has to make the best decision possible for their respective situation with their ex. In some cases, children are involved, property, or other mitigating factors that require some interaction between the two broken-up parties. However, I submit if you must have interaction with your ex and the wounds are very fresh, or the wounds cut very deeply, maintain strong boundaries and support to assist you with coping. If not, further damage could occur to both of you and anyone else connected to the relationship. While many contend that a relationship only affects the two people in it, that is not entirely true. Many couples have children, family members, shared friends, and they attend the same social gatherings where they interact with other people. So, to some degree others are affected by the break-up positively or negatively which is neither here nor there. The ultimate point, the two in the relationship have to decide what is best for them independently and collectively concerning any ongoing connectedness, but perhaps should consider the affects their decision could have on others that may have been pulled into their relationship. It is understood that many choose to remain neutral in matters such as these, but neutral people can be dangerous because they have no definitive ground on what is right or wrong. So, they will go along with whatever is being presented and say, "It is none of my business." Yet, in the same breath they are discussing the relationship with others! So, how neutral or objective are they? As we can see this can be very sticky and tricky as one female responder shared. If you have no reason at all to be connected to an abusive ex perhaps you should not do so?! Closure and healing can be achieved in other ways, so do your best not to get caught up in believing that you have to "talk to" or "hang out" with your abusive ex. For if you do not closely examine your true motives for wanting to remain "cordial" or "friends" you may end up getting burned or tricked. Many, including myself, have experienced this. Be careful! As a quick moment of seeming pleasure could lead to a lifetime of pain; it is not worth it in the end.

Discussion Question: What do you think are some of the *biggest* stumbling blocks that cause romantic relationships to become dysfunctional? Is it insecurities, past baggage, communication etc...? As a matter of fact, how can one tell that the rela-

tionship has the *probability* of being dysfunctional *before* they get all the way invested?

Male Responder: Most people seem to lack the ability to identify those problem areas, or they ignore them. People seem to be jumping in head first and just hoping for the best. Most people don't know what questions to ask or what red flags to look for! A lot of people don't even know what they should and should not accept.

Female Responder: Past baggage. Until one learns to love themselves and know what may have caused them pain and it isn't your fault, forgive, and move forward then they will always carry the baggage.

Male Responder: I'd say all of the above. In my personal experience, insecurities, low self-worth (fear based) and lack of self-awareness are three of the greatest barriers to healthy romantic relationships. Failure to address and heal from abandonment, mommy/daddy issues, trust and self-acceptance render me ill-equipped to participate in healthy relationships. Those dealing with these issues can't hide. I remember dating a woman who had daddy issues and she would subconsciously express her hate for men or talk of how she didn't need a man, but on the flip side of it, she always needed validation from me! The trick to seeing who I'm dealing with is to look at the person through real eyes. Not the lustful eyes, not the codependent eyes, or 'I only see what I want to see' eyes. Remember "Real eyes realize real lies." As for me, I won't engage in sex until we truly get to know one another. Sex has a way of putting blinders on reality.

Female Responder: Trust and communication has always been two important areas in relationships for me. I totally have no tolerance for liars and those who shut down or run from adult dialogue and I agree sex does put another spin on reality!

As we can see this discussion topic from the ***Pimp-A-Lo Syndrome Vol. 1*** created great dialogue. I added much to this discussion as well, as the author. Here are a few of the things that I stated in the discussion, "Some red flags, or signs of the probability that a relationship may become dysfunctional at the beginning stage: The person angers easily, dishonesty, they speak with strong negative emotion and often about their last relationship and they share about their former mate in a negative manner as if they were constantly victimized. They do not follow through on their word and they are too clingy too quickly. The person acts like they have been together in the "getting to know stage" of the relationship 5 years and it's been 5 weeks! They have no ability to disagree, and there may be signs of financial instability. The list of signs can go on and on and on." Ultimately, one must pay attention to their new potential relationship partner, and themselves. Sometimes, the other person may not be the one displaying all of the aforementioned signs. It could be you! Often times, loneliness and desperation can cause a person to dive in completely giving the new connection, that might become a relationship, too much flavor from the onset, and that reader is most certainly a red flag.

The probability of "doing too much" too early into the connection is exceptionally high for persons with addictive personalities. So, if one knows that they have issues with obsession, compulsion, and being totally self-absorbed into what they want, when they want it; this person may want to obtain some coaching on healthy dating, or else risk running the potential relationship partner off. I would like to throw in a few things to consider when meeting someone new:

Do not disclose too much deep personal information about yourself right away. You don't know this individual like that yet!

If you are feeling "weak at the knees" or anywhere else, know that this attraction may be lust only, and may lead you to eventually feeling like you are in hell once the euphoria wears off and you see the individual for who they really are!

Monitor how often you are communicating with this person. On social sites, through phone calls, and yes even text messages.

Observe how much of your time is being spent, mentally, on thinking about this individual. Are thoughts of them consuming your day, and you have only known them for 1 or 2 weeks?

Lastly, if you choose to have sex with them, and it is good, do not assume that you are married, in your mind, in 30 days! Healthy relationships take time to build.

If your behavior or thoughts are anywhere in the "ballpark" of the previously mentioned 5 things to consider; please be aware that you may need more work on yourself & you are emotionally dangerous to you. The previous formula has caused many people to end up in ghastly dysfunctional relationships. So, slow down, pay attention to you, pay attention to the other party, and secure a relationship coach that is relatively healthy. This relationship coach can be: A therapist, A guide from a 12 step program, parents, siblings, someone from your spiritual community, sound friends, or even a colleague that you have that kind of rapport with. In any case, whomever you select to be a relationship coach, ensure as much as reasonably possible, that they are relatively healthy in their relationships and they are not actively doing the previously mentioned 5 things themselves.

Discussion Question: Often times when people are "caught-up" in a dysfunctional relationship and they are truly attempting to break-free they may be met with swift judgment or shaming from others-that may or may not have all of the facts (especially if it triggers unfinished business in them which can cause more damage). What are some ways that one can help without making the person feel "torn down" and "judged"?

Female Responder: I think one of the best things one could do is refrain from "if I were you". Not judge the situation and be a good listener and confidant. Share my experience

14

and give "advice" when asked.

Male Responder: First I believe that the person should be supported even if that person is afraid to get out. Second pray with and for both of the individuals involved. Third don't get caught up in the person's dysfunction.

I truly liked the responses that book group members were giving. I believe all of the responses given on this question would be helpful to an individual that is "caught-up." It is truly a "fragile" time when dealing with an individual that is in a dysfunctional relationship and everyone is "not" equipped to do it. For it can become challenging especially if you are close to the individual! So, often times "less is best" and " a little is more" and "timing" is essential to say anything. To sum up this particular discussion question, many were saying that they would pray with the individual, and not offer "unsolicited advice." I am in total support of persons not offering unsolicited shaming advice, or absolutes such as: You should have, you never, you always, what is wrong with you, are you out of your mind etcetera. Those kinds of statements can push the person into the dysfunction deeper and create deep emotional scarring. So, to avoid this do all you can not to shame or judge someone in a dysfunctional relationship. Now I am not suggesting that you condone the behavior. It is extremely difficult to watch family members, or close friends ersnared in a relationship that is killing them emotionally, mentally, physically, and spiritually. I know this from personal experience on both sides of the spectrum. My suggestion would be "reflective listening" and being emotionally present, as much as reasonably possible, without damaging you! It may be fine to say things like, "It hurts me to see you hurting" or "I am worried about you because I love you and I want to see the best for your life, you just said you want to see the best for your life as well. So how can we get there?" Many times, people speak their own answers if one is "truly" listening to them, instead of trying to fix them! Being that the person in the dysfunctional relationship is already on high-alert; they will pick up easily on any sarcasm, back door under-handed statements of judgment, or self-righteousness. Why? I am glad that you asked! They are living it daily in the dysfunctional relationship. So, they are hyper-vigilant and on edge already and they are typically speaking negative self-talk to themselves daily. They have already judged themselves. For this reason, it is simply not a good idea to shame or judge in hopes that this will make the person leave the romantic relationship, or marriage. If you are unsure on how to be supportive to someone you care about that is caught up in a dysfunctional relationship, ask a professional. Gather free materials on how to support this person. Many domestic violence centers across the country offer these materials free of charge. Also, you can Google this topic and much information will come up that may prove to be helpful.

Discussion Question: Can "great sex" hinder a person from leaving an abusive relationship? Let us keep in mind that abuse does not have to be physical only. It can be mental, emotional, or spiritual. If sex does contribute to a person remaining in unacceptable conditions, what are some "healthy steps" that they may take to break free from a "feeling" that is contributing to their deterioration?

Female Responder: Great sex gives the person a false sense of reality, leaving a person thinking "If we connected on this level, we must be meant to be", Even if there are serious red flags you stay because you think how in the world can I connect to another person on this level. Sex clouds your judgment and gets you wrapped in feelings NOT facts, values, beliefs and convictions. To free yourself from this control through sex, YOU MUST, cease all contact with the person. You must be willing to examine your situation under a microscope and swallow the big pill of dysfunction that was always there and YOU must get help if you can't do it alone. This is going to take you being open and honest with others and willing to have an accountability partner/counselor. You can never control if the other person will change, you have to be willing to make the change.

Male Responder: My experience is that when I found out what truly made me happy, the sex became less important. The entire relationship was based on making the other person happy. The so called "great sex" was only a physical solution to a spiritual problem. So, I wound up with an empty soul and having great sex. What a miserable situation that was.

Female Responder: Yes great sex could for some but not in my case, it was neediness and co-dependency issues I suffered from...because the sex wasn't good! The man had a thimble in his pants, but I thought at the time I could not live without him, or could not make it without him. It was my insecurities, low self esteem, low self worth and abandonment issues that kept me tied to him. It was an unhealthy soul tie. I needed God. I needed a twelve step program and counseling. I had to learn to love myself. I had low self esteem, and no sense of self worth. I thought I did not deserve any better. Once I began working on myself, and rebuilding my value system I learned who I was. I had to change my entire belief system and build up my self esteem and learn to love me. Only then did I believe I deserved better and was able to establish healthy relationships with men, because before then, I attracted who I was at that time. I was very unhealthy, so I attracted toxic people. As I became healthier, I learned the difference between a toxic dysfunctional relationship and a healthy one.

My response as the author to discussion question 5: I want to thank everyone that responded to this type of question. I have witnessed sex be a dominating factor in relationships for both women and men. Other than the sex that a person "can" become addicted to, that is why there is treatment for sexual addiction, the person is not getting what they need otherwise to sustain a healthy relationship! The same dysfunctional dynamic could potentially play out and become equally as dysfunctional if this topic was changed from "sex" to" financial stability." Some people remain in a dysfunctional relationship, or marriage just for financial purposes, but they are being mistreated, which is equally abusive. If a person wants to break free I agree that they would need to surrender and get the "proper" support to walk with them through the process. There are various support groups, individual therapy, and various clinical materials that may assist them. I am very clinically fond of **Dr. Patrick J. Carnes**. He is one of the leading psychologists currently that specializes in sexual addiction, traumatic bonding, and chemical dependency paradigm models. He also has treatment facilities. Hopefully if someone is among us that is in an abusive relationship driven by sex, finances, or other factors they may be encouraged to seek the support they need by reading "all" of the responses given and know that they are NOT alone, others have experienced it and have broken free and if they do the necessary work they can be liberated too."

The purpose of this chapter was to assist readers that may be going through a dysfunctional relationship experience possibly get some help from the experiences of others. This particular discussion question was very extensive and informative, so I would like to suggest that my readers come to my website *www.teenaharrisinitiative.com* and become an active part of my blog. Hopefully you will find some healing there.

Rocked to Sleep Recovery
Chapter 3

Many have seen a new mother or father rocking their newborn baby asleep. I did this when I was a new mother. I was very gentle and nurturing in my rocking. I may have hummed a song to my baby in an attempt to soothe her and assist her with falling asleep. There were times when my baby appeared to be asleep, and the moment that I moved in an attempt to go lay her down, she would awaken! So, I would start the entire process over again until she actually fell asleep. My intentions were pure in rocking my child asleep and she felt safe. Thereafter, I would go and lay her down in her crib, and I would try to get a little rest, or go take care of a few tasks in the house while she slept.

This same process of actually rocking a baby to sleep occurs in unhealthy romantic relationships; inclusive of marriages. The intent of being rocked to sleep is not pure or safe. It is for manipulative purposes only. The objective is for you to be unaware while your mate does unhealthy things that will ultimately create harm for you. While you may not be physically snoozing, you are in fact, consciously slumbering, walking around going through your day with your eyes wide shut. How is this accomplished? I am glad that you asked!

In many cases (not all cases) some get rocked to sleep by great sex and a story of promise and change that is filled with lies in reality. However, the "sleepwalker" does not see this. They are sedated with the spell that their mate has placed on them, or this enchantment was placed upon them from some previous unaddressed abusive traumatic episode. At times, a person is not rocked to sleep by sex, or a story that they are told, instead they are rocked to sleep by the story that they are telling themselves internally to keep them in this altered fantasy state. They tell themselves things similar to this, "My mate is not that bad they do love me, and we will get through this. It will change, I have faith. No one else will want me. We have so much history I cannot see myself without this person." Also the person can be rocked to sleep if their mate treats them well for a couple of weeks or months doing all of the things that were always desired; and once you fall back asleep the relationship goes back to the true dysfunctional state that it was always in; this is a cycle that repeats itself. **It is just like the pattern on the Domestic Violence Wheel of Power and Control referred to as: The Honeymoon Stage.**

Denial is an understatement at this particular juncture in the unhealthy relationship. It is much deeper than denial. The person is pretty much emotionally comatose. The person has typically cut all individuals off that will keep them "awake" meaning in reality and truth. In many cases, the "sleepwalker" will have family feuds with loved ones and close friends that are attempting to assist them with seeing that this relationship is destroying their life. The sleepwalker will become vicious, condescending, defensive, secretive, and dishonest with any person that attempts to give them a dose of reality about their love interest. The "sleepwalker" has fully adopted the fantasy and they believe they cannot live without this relationship. It brings to mind a song by Rose Royce titled, "I'm going down." In this song she is singing about going down all because she is not with this man anymore and her whole world is turned upside down; and she does not want to live. Reader this is a serious unhealthy state of mind that the "sleepwalker" is in, and this can be a man or a woman in this state of mind.

Now the "sleepwalker" is roaming around with no support, with the exception of other "sleepwalkers" that are giving them sedated advice, and they are running into things, while asleep, that could destroy them permanently. This is so serious that it can be metaphorically compared to a person having narcolepsy driving, and they fall asleep at the wheel of their car. If this were to happen they could have a fatal accident that may kill them or someone else. In some cases, when a person falls asleep at the wheel, and they miss having a fatal accident it may be enough to wake them up so that they may get some rest, or help so that a fatality will not occur.

Eventually some event will happen that will finally wake the "sleepwalker" up! The episode that transpires to wake them is typically very shocking to them! Now keep in mind, it may not be shocking to others that have been in reality about this dysfunctional relationship because they knew these things were going to occur and tried to warn them, but they were met with the "sleepwalkers" wrath in the past and could do nothing to stop the train wreck. These are some of the events that could potentially take place to wake the "sleepwalker" up: They may find their lover in bed with someone else. They may look at their bank account and see all their money gone. They may see text messages, or over-hear phone conversations that are hurtful about them. They may contract a venereal disease from their mate. They may discover that their mate was living a double life and they had another lover with children. They may have a serious physical altercation with their mate, or all of the above may occur, which would be rather unfortunate, but the person would be FORCED to wake up; and they will not be happy! The sleepwalker will be emotionally traumatized like a deer in the headlights, and they will have to undergo some form of recovery in an effort to redeem their emotional, mental, spiritual, and physical well-being again.

The recovery process for the "sleepwalker" will be similar to the same process of having medical surgery. If you have ever had surgery reader you are aware that there is a protocol in place for scheduled surgeries, and there is a different process in place for emergency surgeries. There are similarities to both types of surgery, but one is planned and the other is unplanned and crisis related. With scheduled surgery the physician is typically seeing the patient regularly, and they may discover that the patient requires surgery. If the physician determines that the surgery is not until death, but needs to occur, they will:

1. *Have a consultation with the patient about it and this would include asking what is their family history with this illness?*

2. *Inform the patient on what is permissible and not permissible before the procedure.*

3. *Answer any of the patient's questions, and address any concerns about the procedure.*

4. *Then schedule the surgery perhaps 2 weeks out.*

Once this process takes place the patient may be kept inpatient for a couple of days, or it may be an outpatient procedure where the patient is permitted to go home that same day. In either case, once the patient has the procedure they go to the recovery room for a period of time while the anesthesia wears off some and then the patient is discharged and sent home with specific instructions and a follow-up appointment to make sure that things are healing properly.

However, the unplanned crisis surgery has a totally different dynamic. A patient may not have been seeing a physician regularly. Perhaps they have been ignoring a certain pain for quite some time. The potential crisis patient will try to treat themselves with over-the-counter remedies that will provide temporary relief, and believe that they are fine. Then when the pain resurfaces they use more over-the-counter temporary relief remedies, or they get advice from friends that are not physicians, and take their suggestions and things eventually get worse. Now the potential crisis patient has no choice but to go to the emergency room! Perhaps going to the emergency room was not their idea, maybe they fell out and someone called the paramedics. In any case, they are now at an actual hospital for this ignored, self-treated pain that has gotten increasingly worse, and ended in crisis.

So the trauma team is summoned out to assess the patient. They are flying down the hospital hallway to get the patient to the trauma room. The attending ER physician comes in quickly to assess what is going on, nurses are taking blood, orders are given by the ER Physician that this patient "must" have surgery right now, or else death is imminent. The patient may have eaten a meal before they fell out or taken other medications. So, the risk is higher because with planned surgery there are specific plans to follow before a surgical procedure, but in crisis all of those preliminary important factors have to be cast to the wind because this is a crisis. The patient is then:

1. *Injected with various I.V.'s given sedating medication,*

2. *The physician is explaining to the patient, or some loved one what has to take place to spare their life*

3. *The patient is rushed off into surgery for 3 hours, while loved ones wait nervously in the hospital lobby.*

4. *Then the physician comes out and explains to the family that the patient is critical, and is in the recovery room, and visitors are not permitted at this time unless it is immediate family 2 at a time and quickly*

After this emergency surgery has taken place to spare the patient's life and they come to, typically the patient is confused from the anesthesia, looking around trying to establish if it was all a dream or not, and then the physician walks in. At that time, the physician begins to explain the procedure that had to be done to spare their life. Then the physician's ask the patient very basic questions such as, "Were you experiencing any pain before last night? When you experienced this pain did you discuss it with your primary care provider? In what ways were you coping with this pain? What medications have you been taking?" At that time, the patient, out of fear, tells the truth that they have been treating themselves, asking friends how to attend to it, and they have not been to their primary care provider at all because they were scared and they believed that it would just get better. Then the physician informs the patient on how important it is to see their primary care physician regularly & not to take advice from persons that are not their doctor. The physicians then inform the patient that they will be remaining in the hospital for a few days for observation and recovery. While the crisis patient is there family and friends come to visit, perhaps spiritual advisors may come to visit, and the crisis patient begins to reflect on the importance of taking care of their health. The crisis patient is out of immediate crisis and in some realization of their reality and they are more open. After a few days in the hospital, the physician informs the patient that they may be discharged, but they have very specific instructions to follow so that they will not have a set-back. The crisis patient ensures the doctor that they will follow these instructions, attend the follow-up appointment, and thanks medical staff for saving their life.

All that said, when the "sleepwalker" enters into the recovery process from a deeply dysfunctional relationship they are like the crisis medical patient. The only difference is it is emotional, mental, and spiritual. Actually, they may have some physical discomfort from the stress and strain of the relationship, but they are very fragile, but most importantly they are alive and AWAKE. It will be important to those attending to the now awakened "sleepwalker" with care and compassion. This is not to suggest that the person is coddled to the point of rocking them back to sleep, but it is to suggest that you are able to share gentle truth with them one bite at a time as they are healing. Do not be shaming saying, "I told you so. You should have listened to me. A hard head makes a soft behind et cetera" Those statements "will" cause more emotional and spiritual injury. The person is not strong enough yet to deal with too much deep level truth, and when that time comes it should be done in a certain manner out of true care and concern. Parenthetically, there are some people that truly need sensitivity training before they seriously injure another living soul with their harsh abrasiveness that they believe will help when in all actuality they are being more damaging.

Spiritual Nugget

Real recovery has a spiritual component to it for those on a healing journey. There are various spiritual principles that may be applied to aiding someone that is wounded. While many hold different spiritual beliefs, which I have no judgment on for I know who I serve and what I believe in, and there some that are not sure on what to believe spiritually and my hope is that they find the spiritual path of truth in their lives. Yet, I contend that Love is the greatest spiritual principle of all. True and sincere love is not abusive, shaming, or damaging. On the contrary, true spiritual love is healing, redeeming, understanding, compassionate, and wise. So, do your best to spread love and give the truth in compassionate love. Do not create a bigger wound for another person. If you are unsure on how to do this, seek out the experience of those who do, and allow them to teach you of their healing ways. It may prove to be beneficial to you on your journey.

Rocked to sleep recovery is an ongoing process, just like the crisis medical patient and their ongoing care as discussed above. There are specific things that one must do in order to enter into and remain in "recovery" from being rocked to sleep:

1. Obtain accountability partners that will assist with keeping you awake

2. Find a safe place to deal with and process your emotions, thoughts, and beliefs. One may choose to do this in therapy, in support groups, with family, with friends, or with a spiritual guide. However, be careful on who you reveal your pain and recovery to. Investigate a little to make sure that the person has integrity, they are spiritually and emotionally mature, and they are confidential.

3. Attend various 12 step support groups such as: Codependency Anonymous, or Alcoholics Anonymous (Al-Anon). If you have a chemical dependency issue there are many 12 step programs that you may choose to attend. All of these support groups are free, but one must be careful when entering into these various circles of recovery meetings because the people there are trying to get better too, and some are just there. So, obtain a sponsor to assist. Do your homework.

4. Begin to build your spiritual life by prayer and meditation. There are many avenues to explore to do this. There is a vast difference between spirituality and religion. While there are some similarities, spirituality is less about control and more about living by certain principles, such as: humility, honesty, acceptance, willingness, open-mindedness, love, and hundreds of other spiritual principles. Typically, once one starts to practice these spiritual principles they may decide to attend a formal place of worship. My only sugges-tion is to ensure that if you join any organized religious institution do your homework on that establishment so that you are not messed up theologically.

5. Cease all contact with your former mate. If you must have contact with this former mate due to children or financial obligations, use your accountability partners to assist you with support, and keeping your boundaries clear.

6. Be sure to build relationships with people that have relatively healthy relationships themselves. Just because a person is married that does not qualify them automatically to be in a healthy relationship. For the most part, when people are in a relatively healthy relationships, it contains the following qualities: Love and support for one another, true intimacy, honoring one another, praying together, trust; loyalty to one another, shared friends and independent friends, things are done together and separately, the ability to agree to disagree without hurting one another, complimenting one another without los-ing your identity in one another.

These are a few qualities that healthy relationships have. Keep in mind that there are no perfect relationships. Connecting with another person and remaining connected takes work on the part of both individuals. However, there are healthy and unhealthy relation-ships. Ultimately, you will have to decide what is healthy for you.

These are some steps that will assist the person that has been rocked to sleep get into personal recovery concerning their own well-being. As one can see, from the 6 steps men-tioned above, it is truly an active process that takes time and dedication. With this said, it is also possible for relapse to occur if a person that has been rocked to sleep does not remain on their regiment where re-injury can happen, and we will discuss that in the next chapter.

The Emotional & Physical Relapse Process
Chapter 4

In the examples of the routine patient and the crisis patient, in the previous chapter, one of the common themes was follow-up care after their surgery. The purpose of a follow-up appointment, again, is to ensure that the recovering process is happening sufficiently, and if there are any problems the physician can attend to it before it becomes severe. During the follow-up appointment, the doctor may determine that the patient has to: attend physical therapy for 12 weeks, change their diet indefinitely, and take certain medication for their over-all sustainability. The physician may convey to the patient that if they do not heed their medical recommendations, relapse or a set back could occur that may be fatal. Yet, if the patient follows the medical treatment plan, they may live life relatively healthy like others do. Additionally, depending on the severity of what the patient is recovering from, the doctor may strongly suggest that the patient see a therapist or obtain emotional support from family or friends to assist them with coping and staying the course.

At this point, the patient, fresh from the surgery, is fully aware of the importance of doing what the physician is advising them to do. So without delay the patient begins doing everything requested. The patient even has their family or other support persons assisting them with the lifestyle changes that have to be made. Gung-ho, they spring forth with their new regiment. But along the way, a few things will occur that causes them to falter! What are these things? I am glad that you asked!

The patient begins to take these faltering steps:

1. Mentally, they begin to feel better around week 4 or 5. So, they begin to tell them-selves, "I really don't need to do all of this, but maybe some of it." Keep in mind they do not share this with anyone that has been supporting them with staying the course.

2. Emotionally, they begin to feel cocky, over-confident, or even resentful that they must be on this regiment in the first place. So, their patience becomes thin, anger surfaces, and they begin to slowly detach from their support. In the midst of this, they begin to recall how their life was before the surgery, and they silently wish it was the old way.

3. Spiritually, they are not praying as much, if at all, and they may be resentful with a Higher Power or God, saying to themselves, "Why me," or "God can you make it like it was?"

4. Physically, they have now started eating small things they should not eat, they skip a couple of physical therapy session, then ultimately they stop doing all of the mainte-nance required and things seem okay initially. They tell themselves, "See, I knew I did not have to do all of this stuff. I am cool!"

Perhaps, for a few weeks, maybe even a few months, things appear to be fine. Then, one day, they fall out somewhere, and the EMT (emergency management team) is called to the scene! The patient is now in critical care, and the patient does not die, but they feel dead! Once various medical procedures are conducted and the patient is brought back to a level of stability, the physician comes in for the conversation. The first question is typically, "What happened to cause this episode?" The disillusioned patient states, "I have no idea. I was doing everything you suggested and then one day I just fell out!" Then the physician informs the patient, "Due to the damage that your tests reveal, you have not been following the regiment for quite some time! At this point, we are going to refer you to a higher level of inpatient care where we can monitor your progress, and medical decisions will be made accordingly. We apologize, but this has to be done in order for you to live." The patient is now angry, embarrassed, fearful, but thankful that they are alive. They survived this relapse, but have they learned anything?

What we examined above is the process of a medical relapse, but the same thing happens when one relapses emotionally with an unhealthy relationship. It typically does not occur in one day. There are actions that are not taken and taken that contribute to the relapse occurring. It is customary to have an unfulfilled fantasy about the relationship, or having the desire to be "friends," or believing that the person really has changed because "they said so." When you do not discuss these things with your accountability partners, getting back with your ex in any capacity seems like a good idea.

Another scenario can take place that could contribute to relapse. Suppose your ex has a serious life crisis and they contact you because you are the only person that can really help them. So, you dive in, blindly, out of your codependency, and past patterns of doing the same for so long, way back when, with your ex. After assisting them with this crisis your ex is so grateful for your helping them. They express this to you over and over again and tell you those three magic words, "I love you." And you begin to trust those misguided emotions that lead you to believe:

- *You are needed*
- *They do trust you and care about you, because they reached out to you at such a critical time*
- *Maybe the two of you can "work it out"*
- *Maybe others are wrong about you and your relationship. After all, you are a grown up and this is your life, not anyone else's!*

The next thing you know, you are talking to your ex intermittently, not telling others about the communication, and ultimately you have sex with your ex. Now you are living by the lyrics of Anthony Hamilton's song, "Can't Let Go." In the song, he repeats one line, "No matter what the people say I'm going to love you anyway-you are my life I can't let go!" Then you rehash all of those strong emotions and start believing the lies again, and your ex starts back with the SAME shenanigans and you realize nothing has changed! The trick is on you! You begin hearing Vivian Green's song, "Emotional Rollercoaster," and you are like her in the song asking the Lord, "What I have gotten myself into!" You are feeling stupid, angry at yourself, and embarrassed to share it with those that will help you! At this point, you have internalized every unhealthy emotion and thought possible, which is the trick of the enemy! Remember, relapse is spiritual in nature as well; the spirit is typically the first thing to go! In your mind, the last thing you want to hear is, "I told you so!" So, you proceed on, trying to manage this alone for a period of time until some kind of major episode occurs that cannot be ignored; then you are back in critical care again.

Spiritual Nugget

Have you ever taken notice of all the songs about love that are geared toward codependency and not being able to "let go?!?" Many of these songs I like as well. However, it seems like when you have relapsed all of those songs become #1 in your playlist! The songs are rocking you back to sleep, and you are feeling like Musiq in his song, **"Halfcrazy."** Music is healing and powerful, but the wrong message in music can push one deeper into an unhealthy state of mind and nearly put one in a trance. Some readers might think, "Now come on that is not true!" Yet I submit to you that it is! It is the power of persuasion. In my faith, the lower power was the minister of music. God had given him this gift, and he was highly seductive with it once he fell from grace with God. So, he lurks in music to seduce and manipulate. Additionally, what you look at entices you as well. Here is a great example: You are sitting at home watching T.V. and you see the same commercial several times showing you the new burger from McDonald's, and you are not even hungry and on a diet plan. However, looking at this same commercial so many times has given you the subliminal message, "I have to try this sandwich! I am starving!" So, you get up and go to McDonald's and get this burger. Now you are addicted to this sandwich and off of your diet and you put on 10 more pounds! It all started with the first sandwich that you were subliminally encouraged to believe that you needed. I think you are feeling me reader. I have done this as well. So this is why I am suggesting be careful of what you allow into your eye-gate and ear-gate while in recovery from this dysfunctional relationship. If not, it may lead to relapse. You may have to get rid of pictures and other memorabilia that serve as reminders of this relationship because your mind will assist you with romancing the "good times" and set you up! Back to the relapse we go…

For some, this last major episode is enough to break the unhealthy soul-tie, and they take their bruised ego, learn from this relapse, and move forward with their life. For others, they continue to remain in relapse mode out of shame & guilt which could ultimately lead to irreparable damage if continued. This is a very real issue! Many have committed suicide or homicide due to pain like this. One direction leads to a permanent dirt nap, while the other leads to life behind bars! Is this relationship worth this much?

In my first book, I shared a brief synopsis of my story, but it was not the entire story. I had a couple of very painful emotional relapses with my ex. These relapses were not so much physical as they were emotional and spiritual from the "original traumatic bond" that I had with this individual and a very deep spiritual hurt that I had in advance of ever getting into this cycle of dysfunctional insanity. There were some steps I took, at that time, during my "emotional relapse" that may prove to be helpful to you:

- *Assess what triggered, or caused the relapse to occur in the first place with someone qualified to assist.*

- *Develop an action plan to get back on your healing regiment*

- *Cease any and all communication with your ex; unless children are involved or other factors cause some communication. If you require some communication be sure that it is in your action plan on how to do this without causing you or your ex further harm. However, social network sites like: Facebook, Twitter, Instagram, Flicker, or any other social site remove the connection*

- *All memorabilia that is reminiscent of the relationship needs to be removed. For example: Pictures, gifts, videos, trinkets or anything that reminds you of your former relationship partner that is around the house or in your phone. Of course this does not apply to children or if the two of you had a dog together, but other external reminders.*

- *Disconnect from any of your ex's friends so you will not be tempted to ask anything, or having them voluntarily telling you things that keep you connected when you were not even thinking about your ex! Close this door completely! Even if they are shared friends let them go if they were your ex's friend first.*

- *Go into your backyard or some acceptable other place, and have a funeral ceremony. Yes, I said a funeral ceremony. Write one last letter to your ex. Include everything in there that you would like to say and how you feel. Be sure to take a trusted friend along for support if you feel comfortable enough. Perhaps you may choose to read this letter to your trusted friend at the ceremony. Then burn the letter and a picture of you & your ex and say: Ashes to ashes, dust to dust. (Note: please be careful with lighting the paper and picture on fire as not to burn other things. If you are unsure, just tear it up and follow the same steps as listed above)*

- *Thereafter, give yourself permission to "walk through" the stages of grief. This may include: crying, anger, utter disbelief, sadness, depression, and ultimately you will achieve "ACCEPTANCE"*

Once I took the aforementioned actions and did "my work" I was finally set free!!! I finally took the pain from my last emotional relapse personal and I became legitimately angry in a healthy way to take positive action for myself. Did this hurt? Yes it did. Did I die? Obviously not- thank God! Was I bitter? No, I was not. I actually felt a heavy burden lift because I was truly ready for a new chapter in my life. However, I clearly understood that this work was ongoing, and with moving forward I needed to stay the course that fostered growth and not pain. I stopped punishing myself for a serious mistake and I accepted that I was beautifully human prone to the same short-comings as others.

I am unsure of what your emotional or physical relapse has specifically been like for you reader, but I would gather that it has been painful! If you are tired of harming yourself it is my sincere hope that you move past the embarrassment of it all, and allow someone to help you. It will be important to learn something from your relapse, so that you do not repeat it again. Then after you see the pattern and learn the lesson, you may move on with living life. Please keep in mind that your support system will be an instrumental part in assisting you with "getting back on the wagon". Your support system is not there to crucify you; if they are "shaming you" release them, and be open to those on the healing path that God will send to you. Sometimes, those whom may have been helpful in the past simply do not have the objectivity to help you anymore. This is fine and understandable you may need a new fresh perspective! Some time's people's role in your story is over. With this new awareness and fresh perspective we are now ready to move into this new dimension of "your healing work" in the next chapter of this life work.

The 14 Day Workbook/Inventory Guide & Recovery Plan
Chapter 5

"Action is the foundational key to all SUCCESS." (Pablo Picasso)

At this point you may be thinking, "Oh my goodness another workbook!" If this is the case, let me have your permission to encourage you. As the artist Picasso said "Taking action is the key." If you do nothing but become aware of your issue, then you haven't done much of anything at all! I do not profess that my workbook is better or worse than any other workbook out there. I believe that when a person is ready to do "their work" and they are asked the right questions at the right time change can begin.

As previously mentioned, in my own experience I had to do "my work" to start breaking free. In my last book I spoke of a paradigm model that helped me. The model outlined in this book further assisted me with staying the course, and I have used this model for many things even in my professional career. As a matter of fact this model has an integrative approach to the change process. It is called, "The Transtheoretical Model" it was developed by Prochaska and DiClemente in the early 80's. It is called the "Transtheoretical model" because it integrates key constructs from other theories. The TTM describes stages of change, the process of change, and ways to measure change (Singer, 2009). In this model change is discussed in "six" specific stages. Since that time, other clinicians have contributed to this model. It has been used in: smoking cessation, HIV awareness, substance abuse treatment, domestic violence awareness, and in various professional medical trainings. It is most certainly evidence based practice. In other words, it has been proven to be effective if followed according to all the research that supports this therapeutic approach to helping people change.

In my workbook, we are going to examine which stage of change that you are in regarding making a healthy change regarding your unhealthy relationship. Below I will give an overview of all six stages of the Transtheorectical Model of change and in the workbook you may decide where you are on the scale.

Precontemplation: Not seeing a problem

Contemplation: Seeing a problem and considering whether to act or not

Preparation: Making concrete plans to act soon

Action: Doing something to change

Maintenance: Working to maintain the change

Relapse: Resumed old behaviors after spending some time in the Action and Maintenance Stage

There is a chart developed by Prochaska and DiClemente on the next page that shows what this change cycle looks like.

PROCHASKA and DiCLEMENTE PARADIGM MODEL OF CHANGE

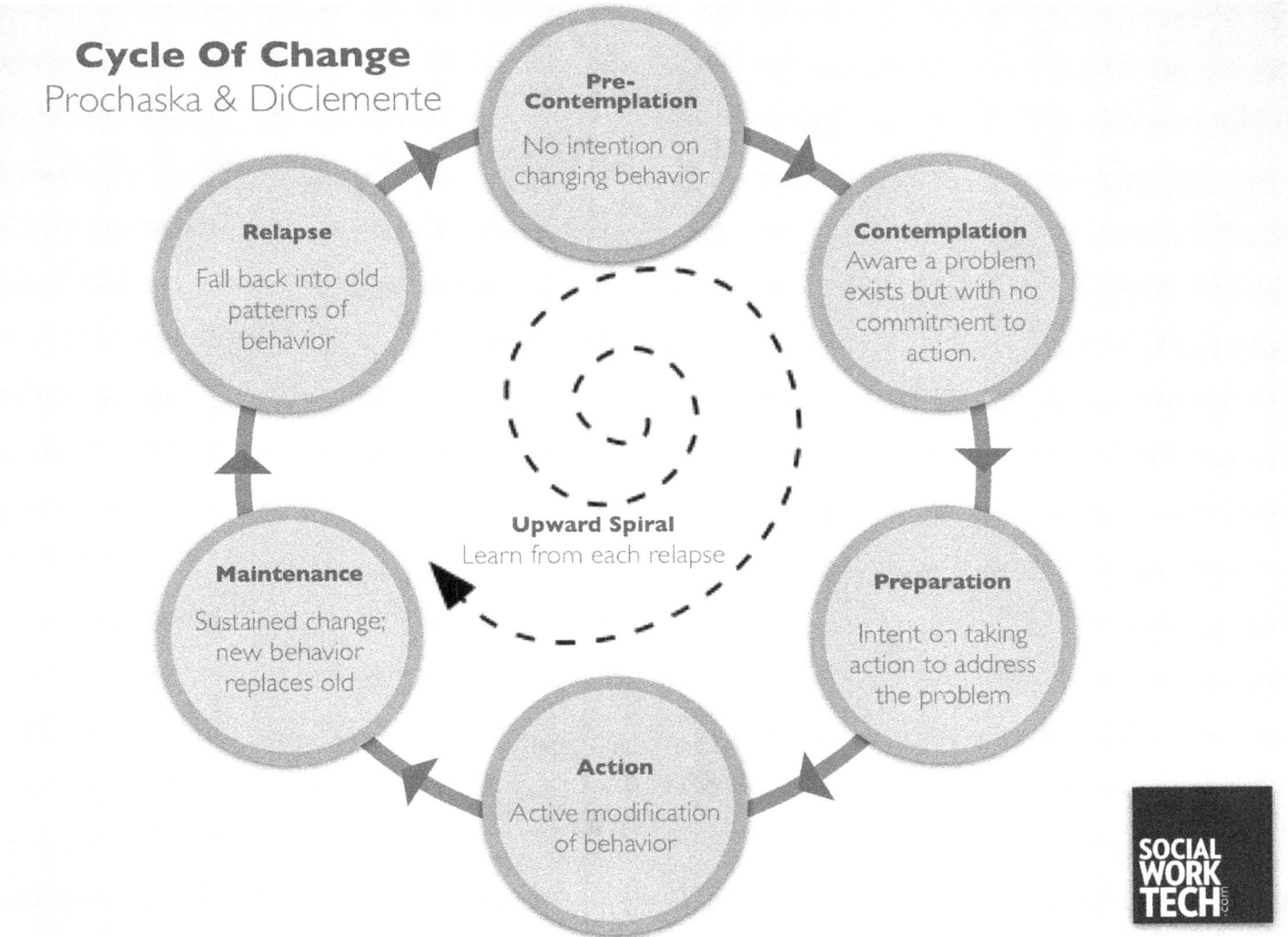

Cycle Of Change
Prochaska & DiClemente

Pre-Contemplation
No intention on changing behavior

Contemplation
Aware a problem exists but with no commitment to action.

Relapse
Fall back into old patterns of behavior

Maintenance
Sustained change; new behavior replaces old

Upward Spiral
Learn from each relapse

Preparation
Intent on taking action to address the problem

Action
Active modification of behavior

SOCIAL WORK TECH.com

Now that you have a visual on what the change cycle looks like it may prove to be helpful as you walk through your change process of breaking free from your dysfunctional relationship. Change is an active process that requires labor. Before we go into the workbook, I am going to provide you with a list of various emotions/feelings that I welcome you to utilize as you express yourself in the workbook. If you do not know what the feeling means I am challenging you to look it up in a dictionary. Remember, "This is your healing process; you worked your way in; and now you must work your way out." This emotions chart is not intended to encompass all the emotions possible, but it is merely a start to some feelings. Often times, emotions drive our decisions and it may prove to be helpful to know which emotions are driving your decisions.

EMOTIONS VOCABULARY CHART

Aggressive	Exhausted	Optimistic	Apathetic	Impressed
Agonized	Frightened	Overwhelmed	Ashamed	Infatuated
Angry	Frustrated	Paranoid	Boastful	Insecure
Anxious	Grieving	Perplexed	Competitive	Insignificant
Apologetic	Guilty	Purlish (sullen or unhappy)		Inspired
Arrogant	Happy	Puzzled	Conniving	Irresistible
Bashful	Horrified	Resentful	Contemptuous	Kind
Blissful	Hot	Relieved	Contented	Lazy
Bored	Hung-over	Sad	Cranky	Loveable
Cautious	Hurt	Satisfied	Delighted	Lustful
Cold	Hysterical	Shocked	Depressed	Martyred
Concentrating	Indifferent	Sheepish	Domineering	Mellow
Confident	Idiotic	Smug	Eager	Nauseated
Curious	Innocent	Surly	Efficient	Nervous
Demure	Interested	Surprised	Egotistical	Noble
Determined	Jealous	Suspicious	Embarrassed	Nonchalant
Disappointed	Joyful	Sympathetic	Enthusiastic	Nostalgic
Disapproving	Lonely	Thoughtful	Expectant	Overworked
Disbelieving	Love-struck	Undecided	Fiendish	Passive
Distastefu	Meditative	Withdrawn	Forgetful	Pressured
Ecstatic	Mischievous	Worried	Gossipy	Scheming
Enraged	Miserable	Grateful	Helpless	Tempted
Envious	Negative	Greedy	Homesick	Tired
Exasperated	Obstinate	Helpful	Hopeful	Worried

Wisdom Nugget

Note to the reader: This is your book & your work. I will provide you with some lines to answer the questions right here in the book, but it may be required that you secure another notebook because you may have more to say on the questions asked. I want to strongly encourage you to keep your book in a *safe place*. Do not leave it lying around somewhere.

It could become unhealthy for you or others if they discover your personal thoughts. You only want to share this work with: Your therapist, counselor, trusted guide, trusted spiritual advisor, or a trusted family member or friend when "you" are ready. Preferably someone that is clinically trained, therapeutically sound, spiritually balanced, honors confidentiality, and understands the process that you are embarking upon. It would be great if this person has the experience themselves and they can share it with you. In any case, this is not something that just any person should hear if you choose to share it. Some of you may complete this workbook and move directly into action, while some may require more support. In either case, it is fine. I want to commend you for making the 14 day commitment, walking through any fears, and being willing to do this work. If it becomes overwhelming for you take a small break, go for a walk, pray, or talk to a friend, but finished what you started. After all, YOU hold the greatest asset and tool to "breaking free" inside of you.

I will start each workbook day off with a thought that I have. Prayerfully it will inspire you to look a little deeper. **Please keep in mind that my workbook is not an ironclad guarantee that you will break-free.** My workbook is simply a catalyst that may assist you with making the best possible decision for your own life and that choice will come from you.

The Workbook / Inventory Guide

Day 1: Assessing my Situation

"Taking an honest inventory of your relationship may truly help you with making a healthier decision, if you remove much of the emotion as reasonably possible and list the facts" (Harris, Teena)

1. What aspects of the previous chapters jumped out to you the most and why?

_____

_____

_____

2. What do you see as your biggest problem in your current relationship; or your past relationships that fit this syndrome? Is it a pattern?

_____

_____

_____

3. What are you accepting, allowing, or accommodating that permits this relationship to continue?

_____

_____

_____

4. What is your role in the relationship victim, rescuer, or persecutor? *Keep in mind one can play all three roles in one scene as discussed in my first book.*

_____

_____

_____

Write a summary on: "How you believe you got into this unhealthy relationship with yourself first and then your mate."

_____

_____

_____

_____

Day 2: Fantasy or Reality

"Do you find yourself imagining or daydreaming that things were better in this relationship, and you prefer being in the daydream about how you wish it was?" (Harris, Teena)

1. In what specific ways are you escaping into fantasy to avoid the reality of your relationship? For example: Are you telling yourself it is not that bad and resting on false hope that it will get better? Are you using chemical substances (alcohol or drugs inclusive of prescription medications)? Are you romancing, in your mind, when things were good in this relationship even if it was a very long time ago?

_____

_____

_____

2. There are typically "3" sets of voices that assists one with keeping a fantasy story going: Your voice, your lovers voice, and the avenues you select to seek information about concerning your relationship. Which of these "3" sets of voices are speaking the loudest to you keeping you in this relationship? What is the story you are hearing?

_____

_____

_____

3. What is the main thing that you keep telling yourself over and over that you believe that keeps you in fantasy about this relationship? For example: No one will want me but this person. I have body image issues that only they will accept. I will never love again? Is it really true?

_____

_____

_____

_____

Write a summary on: "The actual day to day "facts" of what is happening in your relationship." For example: If you are not being treated with love, respect, honor, consideration, compassion, or healthy communication. If things are truly hurtful for you 5 days out of a 7-day week, is this really what you want for your life?

_____

_____

_____

_____

Day 3: Dealing with Anger

"There is a difference between drama and true anger. Drama is slashing tires, making public scenes, or being otherwise messy. True anger motivates people to do something differently in a positive way. For instance, during the Civil Rights Movement various leaders became legitimately angry and began to take a stand in a "positive way" to affect change for the betterment of their lives and the lives of others." (Harris, Teena)

1. Have you truly gotten angry yet? If not, how are you burying the anger you feel? *For example: Are you being passive-aggressive, being sarcastic, creating drama, complaining to friends and family, or sitting in the anger saying nothing when perhaps taking a healthy stand for yourself may prove to be exceptionally helpful for you?*

_____

_____

_____

2. Does anger frighten you? How have you dealt with anger in the past or seen anger dealt with by your parents, family members, friends, or lovers in your life?

_____

_____

_____

3. What is the root of your anger with yourself and what is the root of your anger with your mate?

_____

_____

_____

4. What is causing you to be angry with family or friends concerning your romantic relationship? Have you fallen out with anyone? If so, who & why?

_____

_____

Write a summary on: "How you deal with anger that you have internalized (held in)? Do you over-eat, under-eat, spend money, or deflect by getting into other peoples affairs? Do you become sarcastic or otherwise vicious with people? What does your anger "look like" _____

_____

_____

_____

Day 4: Coping with Shame & Guilt

"Sometimes we can believe that we are "bad" or "stupid" because of poor decisions that we have made. This is not true! If we are making poor choices it does not mean that we are bad or stupid, but it may simply mean we need to learn how to make healthier decisions, and since we can learn and love we are not stupid, or bad- just human." (Harris, Teena)

1. What are the negative self-talk message that you are giving yourself about you and your romantic relationship? For example: Are you telling yourself I don't deserve any better? Are you telling yourself I am getting just what I deserve from the things I have done in my life? Are you telling yourself I am stupid or crazy? *(This question deals with self-worth and self-esteem)*

_____

_____

_____

_____

2. Now that you have identified the negative self-talk messages that you are giving yourself how do you plan on addressing it? If it is true are you willing to change it?

_____

_____

_____

Assignment: *Create "10" positive affirmations about yourself and say them in the mirror looking yourself in the eyes when you say them. Do this for "7" days in a row twice a day, in the morning and at night before bed.* Affirmations are very powerful messages that assist with building self-esteem and uprooting those old self-defeating messages that one may be giving themselves. Affirmations provide empowerment! When you first began to say them it may not "feel" authentic, but if you continue to practice them eventually you will start to believe your affirmations. Mirror work is powerful and healing. **Face yourself, the person you are running from.** Here are a few examples of positive self-affirmations, but I would like to strongly encourage you to create your own affirmations. Positive things you would like to "believe" about yourself.

Examples:
- *I am worthy of the very best life has to offer me*
- *I deserve respect and love*
- *God loves me*
- *I am enough*

Day 5: Overcoming the "I can't help its"

"Many times, as people, we choose the victim role because somewhere subconsciously there is a belief that if nothing can be done about a matter then it must just be destined to be that way! This belief is untrue! One can make solid decisions that can change their life for the better even if it is uncomfortable for a while. So, do not buy that old lie that nothing can be done." (Harris, Teena)

1. Do you find yourself saying things such as, "I can't help it I just love this person and I can't leave them alone?" Is this true, or are you simply unwilling to leave them alone?

_____

_____

_____

_____

_____

2. Have you accepted that you have a choice? What does having a choice mean to you?

_____

_____

_____

_____

3. Do you distrust yourself to make choices? If so, why? What happened that caused you not to trust yourself?

_____

_____

_____

_____

Write a summary on: "How you may start "consciously practicing" exercising your choices and how this may benefit your life, and how you permit yourself to be treated by others. Remember, "There is power in a choice and by continuing to choose to do nothing at all you have in fact made a choice."

_____

_____

_____

_____

_____

_____

Day 6: Dealing with Resentment and Being Offended

"Most can identify with reliving a painful experience over and over again-just recycling the pain far after it has taken place. The experience could be 5 years old, but to the offended person it is as if the event occurred yesterday. Living offended and on edge is like an abscess on your soul. It is very painful and keeps one stuck in misery and discord." (Harris, Teena)

1. After writing on days 1 through 5 what are you most resentful about? What experience are you rehearsing repeatedly in your words and thoughts that show up in your actions?

_____

_____

_____

_____

_____

2. Who has offended you the most in your respective situation? Has it been family, friends, or your mate? What did the person specifically do to offend you? Also, what is the pay-off that you are receiving from rehearsing this pain over and over again?

_____

_____

_____

_____

_____

Write a summary on: "How you plan on learning to forgive yourself and others and stop telling the story over and over again from a victimized place?"

_____

_____

_____

_____

_____

_____

_____

Day 7: The Struggle

"Learning to truly let go when one is accustomed to fighting to hold on to everything can be very challenging! It is as if a tug-of-war is occurring inside of you, and it feels as though you are being torn apart. Oh but beloved, the growth and change is inside the struggle and if you don't give up you will be victorious and no longer a victim." (Harris, Teena)

1. What are the current struggles that you are dealing with now from answering the previous questions?

_____
_____
_____
_____

2. What do you "believe" is going to be the most difficult thing to overcome regarding your unhealthy relationship decision? Are you afraid?

_____
_____
_____
_____

Write a summary on: "How frustrated, annoyed, bitter, sad, defeated, unhappy, or enraged that you feel inside at this point." This is your "getting it out moment." For if you have been truly sticking to the work in this book and answering honestly from your heart, and getting in touch with "your truth," I am highly inclined to believe that you have some uncomfortable emotions going on! If so please know that it is "normal". You are human! My suggestion is to find a safe person to speak with after you write this summary to process your thoughts and feelings with. For example: A 12 step guide, friend, counselor, or a spiritual mentor. Remember, "Make sure that the person you select to share your feelings with has emotional and spiritual maturity." If you believe that you cannot trust sharing with people that you know "right now" use one of the hotline numbers that I provided in the Appendix section of my workbook, and speak to a confidential professional for free over the phone.

_____
_____
_____
_____

Day 8: Walking Through the Change Process

"There will be some rainy days as you are changing, but there will be some sunshine as well. Be gentle with yourself as you have probably gotten in touch with some deep truth about you that previously you were unaware of that will take time to change if it is deeply rooted. Change takes practice, practice, and more practice." (Harris, Teena)

1. Which stage of change are you in about your relationship at this point? Precontemplation, Contemplation, Preparation, or Action?

_____

_____

_____

_____

_____

2. Do you still have "hope" that things will turn around for the better in this unhealthy relationship that you have been in? If so, what are you telling yourself, or hearing that is encouraging you to believe this?

_____

_____

_____

_____

_____

Write a summary on: "How many times you believed that this relationship was going to change, but it did not happen or last." Be sure to include how you "felt" about the disappointment you experienced when the change did not happen or last. Use real emotions from the emotions vocabulary chart provided in this workbook.

_____

_____

_____

_____

_____

Day 9: Accountability Partners

"Some of the greatest battles in history have been won by: Leaders with intelligent strategy for warfare, the element of surprise, and a well trained strong front line & soldiers. The same concept rings true for accountability partners. These are people that have wisdom, integrity, they understand emotional and spiritual warfare, and they have overcome battles. If you enlist these kinds of people into your healing journey you have a higher probability of winning your battle." (Harris, Teena)

1. Have you selected at least "2" accountability partners that may assist you in staying in reality and moving forward in life? If not, do you have "2" people in mind? If so, do these individuals have: integrity, wisdom, emotional & spiritual maturity, experience, and they are confidential?

_____

_____

_____

_____

2. What other "forms" of support are you comfortable using during this time to help you? For example: church, support groups, counseling, or treatment even.

_____

_____

_____

_____

Write a summary on: "How you honestly "feel" about allowing others to help you and what your experience has been like with asking for help?" Be sure to include any fear, embarrassment, or other feelings that you have about needing some support. Something to consider: Do you believe that you can do this alone?

_____

_____

_____

_____

Day 10: Learning to Like You Again

"Often times when we allow others to mistreat us we begin to not like ourselves very much and we send ourselves very negative messages about who we are. As the healing process takes place, one must typically learn to like self again and ultimately love self again. People that have a healthy love for self do not allow others to mistreat them, because they do not mistreat themselves." (Harris, Teena)

1. On Day 4 you were encouraged to write "10" positive affirmations about yourself and say them in the mirror for "7" days. Today would be day "6" of doing so. Have you been doing this? If not, why? If so, how do you "feel" when you say these affirmations to yourself?

_____

_____

_____

_____

2. What do you "believe" about you? Is this belief positive or negative? If this belief is unhealthy could it be contributing to your remaining in an unhealthy relationship, or continuing to attract unhealthy relationships?

_____

_____

_____

_____

_____

Write a summary on, "What are some ways that you may start treating you better? For example: Taking yourself to dinner, taking yourself to the park, or treating yourself to a massage.

_____

_____

_____

_____

_____

_____

_____

Day 11: Dealing With Your Mate

"If you are actively in an unhealthy relationship you may be experiencing some serious challenges while you are trying to establish your healing process. Be encouraged to seek the path of least resistance if you are living with your mate." (Harris, Teena)

1. Is your mate beginning to notice a change in you? If so, what kinds of things are they saying to you and how do you feel about what is being said to you? Do you need a safety plan?

_____

_____

_____

2. If you are not actively with your mate anymore, or living with your mate are you trying to "show" them how much you are changing?

_____

_____

_____

3. After doing some personal inventory work, when you think about your mate what are your feelings about him or her now?

_____

_____

_____

4. Do you believe that your mate has power over you? If so, is this power real or imagined? If it is real what can you do to take your power back? For example: Becoming gainfully employed, attending support groups for your empowerment, moving into your own apartment etcetera.

_____

_____

Write a summary on, "How you may begin to lift your self-esteem and allow others to assist you in doing this to decrease the power that you believe your mate has over you." Also, be sure to include your thoughts on healthy ways to cope with the children if kids are involved.

_____

_____

_____

Day 12: Things to Consider

"Matters of the heart can be very complicated, especially when one in unsure on what they want. In many cases, the parties involved in the dance-with- unhealthy intimacy do not consider the "big picture" and how this dysfunction could affect not only their lives, but the lives of others." (Harris, Teena)

1. If you continue to remain in this unhealthy relationship what is the worst thing that could happen to you?

_____

_____

_____

2. If something were to happen to you who would be affected by it? Would it be your parents, your children, your relatives, or close friends? What kind of damage could this unhealthy relationship create in the ones you love?

_____

_____

_____

_____

3. Have you given any thought to healing the relationships of those whom you love? As they have been watching you go through much pain and it hurts them as well. Perhaps you have had arguments or complete falling outs with them and you were wrong.

_____

_____

_____

_____

Write a summary on, "How you "feel" about some of your past unhealthy responses to loved ones regarding your relationship." Be sure to include how you plan on beginning to forgive yourself and work with your loved ones to restore the relationship. In other words, how do you see this healing occurring? What are you willing to do on your part?

_____

_____

_____

_____

Day 13: Living Beyond the Pain

"As human beings when we are in pain we may believe that this pain will last forever, and we will never get beyond it. This cannot be true because nothing last forever. I submit to you that there is a full life after the pain- sunshine after the rain." (Harris, Teena)

1. What do you imagine that your life would look like and how you would feel if you were not caught-up in this unhealthy relationship with yourself and your mate? What kind of things would you be doing, starting, or completing?

_____

_____

_____

_____

2. Is there anything positive that you can do, while coping with the initial pain that you feel from this relationship that will channel the pain into something healthy to make it more bearable for you? For example: Going back to school, writing a book, starting a business, or taking dance lessons? Some healthy distractions are great while healing.

_____

_____

_____

_____

Write a summary on, "The dreams that you abandoned while spending your time and energy in this dysfunctional relationship." Be sure to include how you may begin to actively pursue your lost dreams and allow your pain to motivate you to do so. You have gone through much and survived so there must be a higher purpose for your life. Are you willing to explore it and possibly help others?

_____

_____

_____

_____

_____

_____

_____

Day 14: Pressing Forward

"It is common, these days, for many to say "keep it moving." Which is easier said than done in many instances, but ultimately moving is the goal or one will never grow. However, there must be motivation, encouragement, planning, and support to "keep it moving" Are you now equipped with the tools to "start moving"? (Harris, Teena)

1. After working through the last "13" days of this workbook do you believe that there is the remote possibility that you can get past this relationship? If not, why not? If so, explain how.

_____

_____

_____

_____

_____

2. Do you believe that you need to let this relationship go? For at the end of the day, this is your decision. What do you want to do?

_____

_____

_____

_____

_____

The last part of the "14" day workbook/inventory is the "Recovery Plan" example that I will outline on the next page. It is my suggestion that you get a separate sheet of paper and follow the outline for the type of "Recovery Plan" that you may require in your respective situation. The ultimate purpose of developing a recovery plan is to move one from where they are currently to where they would like to be. As previously mentioned, recovery plans may vary per the individual and what they are attempting to achieve. However most recovery plans have these basic components:

- The primary problem
- The short-term goal
- The long-term goal
- The method of intervention for achieving these goals
- Each aspect has a time frame and can be measurable

Example Recovery Plan

Name: *John or Jane Doe (Put your name here)*

Primary Problem: *I want to leave this unhealthy relationship that is draining me emotionally, mentally, financially, and spiritually.*

The Short Term Goal: *To secure housing in a safe environment, perhaps with family or friends, physically away from my mate.*

The Long Term Goal: *To get an apartment, maintain gainful employment, stay free of this unhealthy relationship and any other unhealthy relationships, and continue to use my support system.*

Method of Intervention for Short-Term Goals:
- *I will begin to gather any important documents and other pertinent items and place them in a P.O. Box within 1 week.*

- *I will speak with family or friends about my temporarily residing with them until I get on my feet, and I will have this done in 2 weeks.*

- *I will disconnect from my mate on all social sites: Facebook, Twitter, or Instagram immediately when I move out in 2 weeks.*

- *I will attend support groups or secure a therapist to help me cope with my emotions. I will attend support groups once a day daily for 90 days, and secure a Therapist within 30 days.*

Note: *All of the methods are "action" oriented with specific time frames, and can be measured because it produces evidence. Granted some things may not go precisely as planned, but having an action plan is more effective than not having one, and hoping and wishing that* *things will change.*

Method of Intervention for Long-Term Goals:

- *I will continue working and saving my money and get an apartment in 6 months*
- *I will continue to speak with my spiritual guide or mentor daily for ongoing support*
- *I will continue to see my Therapist every 2 weeks*
- *I will be back in college within 1 year*

Reader, I am inclined to believe that you have the point here of my "generic example" of a "Recovery Plan." Action has to be taken to affect change if you have been caught-up in dysfunction of any kind. Perhaps you may want to seek the assistance of someone qualified, or great at planning to assist you with developing your plan, but ultimately you must have a regiment if you want to break-free. Parenthetically, the primary problem could be a safety concern or some other major immediate concern and in that case the short-term goals would change to suit your specific needs. For this reason, I am strongly encouraging you to utilize the resources provided in the Appendix section of this book, so that you may get the best plan of action for your respective situation. It is my position that I would like all of my readers to follow all legal and safety protocols in your city or state when making your decision to break free.

In my professional career, I have worked with my clients on many different treatment plans for their care and the context was professional. In those cases, many of the plans where highly effective, but I submit that no plan is effective if the person that the plan is for is not "bought into" the plan. So, your willingness will be required.

From the Heart of the Author

I am passionate about many things in life. One of the things that I am passionate about is relationships; matters of the heart. It is my position that platonic relationships are equally important as romantic relationships. While the dynamics are a little different in each the connectedness of the heart is essentially the same. So, I encourage others to examine their platonic relationships and romantic relationships. Many times the same patterns unmask themselves. ***When one has a broken heart it takes prayer, time, change, and healthy connectedness to heal that broken heart; in my personal experience. It is not an overnight healing event!*** So be gentle with yourself, your forgiveness process of self andyour former mate, and with family and friends. A whole village is affected from an unhealthy relationship, just as it is with a healthy relationship.

As I discussed in my previous book, I have been heart-broken and have made mistakes in the love department. Just like one of my favorite singers, **Sade,** sang in her song titled "**I'm a Soldier of Love**", I am too a 'Soldier of Love' all the days of my life as her lyrics state in the song. I will continue to practice at loving myself and others. I have written the books that I have because I believe in discovering your truth and healing. I am also keenly aware that many want to be loved and we settle for less. Many of us do not truly know what love really is, or how to go about accepting it, or giving it to another. It is a learning process. It is my sincere hope that a part of my heart touches your heart and fosters healing for you if you have been heart-broken. Please know that you are not alone and eventually you will love again one day, and be loved back with the same measure that you give love; that is if you believe. I am closing out this small section concerning my heart with a scripture that I believe in that comes from my personal faith. In this scripture it describes love. If love is not looking anywhere similar to this description it "may" not be love at all; it may be pure lust and infatuation:

" Love is patient, love is kind. It does not envy, it does not boast, it is not proud. It does not dishonor others, it is not self-seeking, it is not easily angered, it keeps no record of wrongs. Love does not delight in evil but rejoices with the truth. It always protects, always trusts, always hopes, always perseveres. Love never fails…" (1 Corinthians 13:4-8 A portion, NIV)

Suggested Reading:
1. *"The Betrayal Bond Breaking Free of Exploitive Relationships" By: Patrick J. Carnes, PhD.*
2. *"Facing Love Addiction: Giving Yourself the Power to Change the Way You Love" By: Pia Mellody*

May healing and positive energy be upon you as we journey together through living life and connecting with others…

My Best,

Teena

ACKNOWLEDGEMENTS

There are unique people in my life that have blessed me, carried me, and continue to teach me that I honor. I must thank them for supporting my dreams and my work.

I want and need to thank my Mother, Minister L. Dudley. She has been the wind beneath my wings, my prayer covering, my best-friend, my corrector, my protector, a shoulder to cry on, and so much more. Language is truly inadequate to speak to all that my Mother means to me.

I want and need to thank my sister and manager J. Brown. Her limitless knowledge and professional experience has blessed me. Additionally, I admire my sister's strength. Her love knows no bounds when it comes to our family. She has always believed in me.

I want to acknowledge my nephew, little brother, and the son I never had our beloved, "Adam Terrell Harris" who was brutally murdered on September 4, 2009. He was full of love, gifted in sports, danced his butt off, and he loved his family. His mere presence alone would light up any room. His death is one of the thing's that took me to the darkest most traumatic place of my life which set the stage for me to make very unhealthy decisions that nearly ruined my life. However, remembering his voice in my pain, and his love " for the program" is what helped me pull through & inspired me to write this book. Adam, you were right,"We are all we got" that is something that he used to say about our family.

I want and need to thank my daughter, niece, and nephew: Akeya', Janae, and Jamey who is also an author, and a major part of my inspiration. Their resiliency and love of me has kept my arms up on many days when I was tired. They leave the legacy for our family and I am so proud of them all. They are my heart.

I want to thank my darling, darling, Baby London…She is my heart's joy and just the thought of her melts my heart. I am so glad that God blessed our family with her after we have had so much loss. She is the new life.

I want and need to thank my spiritual sisters: C. Horton, R. Jenkins, P. Gant, and J, Jefferson for being on the front row of my life for nearly 19 years. These women are true spiritual divas and I have learned much from them on my journey. They are my accountability partners. I want and need to thank the powerful, loving, and sincere 12 step members that have cheered me on and supported me. You all will always hold a unique place in my heart and life. There are certain members, and you know who you are, that have been there for me in the midnight hour, prayed for me, shared your experiences with me, and helped me to see the bigger picture.

I would like to thank Mr. Bruce George, co-founder of Russell Simmons' Def Poetry Jam, for his insight, coaching, and priceless friendship.

Lastly, I would like to thank my ex... Yes, I said that. People come into our lives to teach us things about ourselves and to show us the work that we must do. He has been one of my best educators that made me a better woman. I wish him the best in his life journey and I pray that all of his dreams come true according to God's perfect will for his life.

APPENDIX: RESOURCES

These are general resources that may prove to be helpful to you in your healing journey if you select to utilize these resources. It is not my intention to suggest that these resources are guaranteed to change your life. The intent is to inform you of options that are available to assist you should you decide to partake in any of these organizations services.

Al-Anon/Alateen Hotline: 800-344-2666
Al-Anon provides help for people who are the relatives and friends of a problem drinker.

Childhelp National Child Abuse Hotline: 800-4-A-CHILD (800-422-4453)
The Childhelp National Child Abuse Hotline is dedicated to the prevention of child abuse. The Hotline offers crisis intervention, information, literature, and referrals to thousands of emergency, social service, and support resources.

Codependency Anonymous Meetings and Support (800-662-HELP or 4357) www. Coda.org

NAMI Helpline 800-950-NAMI (800-950-6264) www.nami.org
National Alliance for the Mentally Ill staffs this information line 9 a.m. to 4:45 p.m. Monday through Friday. NAMI shares information about mental health issues and provides referrals to support groups and educational programs.

National Domestic Violence Hotline 1-800-799-SAFE (7233)1-800-787-3224 (TDD)
Staffed 24 hours a day by trained counselors who can provide crisis assistance and information about shelters, legal advocacy, health care centers, and counseling.

National Drug and Alcohol Treatment Referral Service 800-662-HELP (800-662-4357)
This is not a hotline, but a referral service.

Rape, Abuse, and Incest National Network: 800-656-HOPE (800-656-4673) or www.rainn.org
RAINN operates The National Sexual Assault Hotline in partnership with 1,100 rape crisis centers across the nation, providing free, confidential advice 24/7. RAINN also operates The National Sexual Assault Online Hotline.

Sex and Love Addicts Anonymous. www.slaafws.org (800) 928-9139

BIBLIOGRAPHY

Green, Vivan. Emotional Rollercoaster Album. Released in 2003 by: Columbia. Song referenced from this album, "Emotional Rollercoaster."

Hamilton, Anthony. Ain't Nobody Worryin Album. Released in 2005 by: So So Def & Zomba. Song referenced from this album, "Can't let Go."

Harris, Teena. The Pimp-A-Lo Syndrome; The Cross Between A Pimp & A Gigalo Vol. 1. Norfolk, VA: Loyalty Fam, 2014

Musiq. Halfcrazy/Caughtup Album. Released in 2002 by: Def Soul. Song Referenced from this album, "Halfcrazy."

Pablo, Picasso. (2009). Paintings, Quotes, and Biography. Retrieved from: http://www.pablopicasso.org/quotes.jsp

Sade. "Solider of Love Album. Released in 2010 by: Sony Music Entertainment, RCA Records. Song Referenced from this album, "Solider of Love."

Singer, J. B. (Host). (2009, October 10). Prochaska and DiClemente's Stages of Change Model for Social Workers [Episode 53]. Social Work Podcast. Podcast retrieved Month Day, Year, from http://socialworkpodcast.com/2009/10/prochaska-and-diclementes-stages-of.html

Zondervan NIV Study Bible. (2002). Scripture Reference Corinthians. Grand Rapids, Michigian: Zondervan

www.ingramcontent.com/pod-product-compliance
Lightning Source LLC
Chambersburg PA
CBHW081341090426
42737CB00017B/3239